MW00647570
PICTUREBOOK
MAKERS
SKETCH BY KITTY CROWTHER

PICTUREBOOK MAKERS

English-language edition first published in 2022 by dPICTUS.
Project originated with publisher Lilla Piratförlaget, Stockholm.
Published in Swedish as *Bilderboksmakare*.
lillapiratforlaget.se

A catalogue record for this book is available from the British Library.

Printed in Estonia.

ISBN: 978-1-73997-920-1

Edited by Sam McCullen
Designed by dPICTUS
Cover illustrations by Jon Klassen

dPICTUS helps outstanding picturebooks cross borders and reach new readers around the world. Through our various initiatives, an active community of publishing professionals promote their picturebook projects, discover emerging talent, secure translation rights, and make new publishing connections around the world.

We're based in the South of England and Belgium.

hello@dpictus.com

dpictus.com
picturebookmakers.com

PICTUREBOOK MAKERS

SKETCH BY ISOL

dPICTUS

Introduction

Picturebooks are flourishing. In recent years, the production quality and innovative approaches to picturebook creation have soared, with picturebook makers and publishers around the world continually pushing the boundaries of the form. Concerns in the industry that traditional printed picturebooks were in danger of being replaced by screens have now gone, and an increasing number of contemporary, multi-layered picturebooks are now being enjoyed not only by young children, but by readers of all ages.

During this time, there has also been a growing interest in the process of picturebook making: the stories behind the stories. dPICTUS launched the Picturebook Makers blog in 2014 to give some of the world's finest contemporary picturebook makers a platform to share the deep work that goes into the creation of their books. The artists who feature on the blog are not interviewed; they're just asked to tell the stories of how their picturebooks came to be. The resulting blog posts are wildly varied and fascinating. In this book, we meet twelve of these picturebook makers who, with great generosity, share their experiences, challenges, doubts, sketches, illustrations, and invaluable insights into their creation process.

There is thankfully no formula or step-by-step process to create a successful picturebook. Portuguese publisher Planeta Tangerina puts it this way: "On the table there are different ingredients and a thousand ways of mixing them. And better still, no fixed recipes. Everything is open; everything is possible." So while we can certainly learn from and be inspired by these contemporary picturebook makers – as they learnt from and were inspired by the picturebook makers who came before them – ultimately, we must all take our own path in creation. About this, Beatrice Alemagna says: "I love avoiding walls or barriers, not worrying about age limits, time limits, precise aesthetic rules, pre-established conventions... I always work with something from within, which is strong and expresses itself very clearly and intensely."

The picturebook is a unique and dynamic art form where words and pictures can contradict, subvert and expand upon each other, creating endless opportunities to convey message and meaning in ironic, humorous and altogether unexpected ways. When the words and the pictures communicate different things at the same time, a third reality is created in the mind of the reader – Jon Klassen has referred to this as the "middle spot" – and it's here where magic can happen. As a picturebook maker, it's essential to leave space for the collaborative role of the reader. Shaun Tan says: "You want to invite the reader through the door without telling them where they are."

In the creation process, the words and pictures often evolve together, and many picturebook makers have talked about the importance of being open to surprises – like going for a walk without knowing your destination and not being afraid to get a little lost. Eva Lindström says that "the work itself, how it proceeds, makes things

SKETCH AND ILLUSTRATION BY BEATRICE ALEMAGNA

happen. Along the way I see options; the story has suggestions. I can follow these suggestions, and one thing opens up to something else." Manuel Marsol believes that "accidents in the process provide a freshness that is impossible to achieve intentionally."

The creative possibilities are immense, and we're seeing more and more self-referential picturebooks where the physicality of the book itself plays a central role. Suzy Lee says: "Sometimes, the motivation for creating a book can come from the conditions of the book's structural form and not only from literary subjects." Wordless picturebooks are becoming more prevalent too, as are crossover picturebooks, which sit somewhere between graphic novels and the traditional picturebook.

Picturebooks have the power to convey universal sentiments and challenging themes in deceptively simple ways, engaging with the hearts and minds of readers directly and concisely. Chris Haughton says: "It's been drilled into me that I need to simplify everything to communicate something elemental – so I try to find the very essence of a story and strip everything else back." The art of simplicity in picturebooks is very difficult to achieve, and through resources such as the Picturebook Makers blog, more people are now discovering the complex and time-consuming work that happens behind the scenes, in service of the stories and the readers.

The picturebook makers you'll meet in this book are internationally acclaimed and their outstanding picturebooks are loved by readers all around the world. But what makes their picturebooks so special? Kitty Crowther says: "Luckily, we just don't know. No recipe. But I do believe in honesty. I do believe in art. And to have good art, it needs to come from far away. You need to dig deeply. Even if the story looks simple."

This book is intended for publishing professionals, illustration students, and anyone else with a passion for picturebooks and a curiosity about the different approaches taken to make them. I hope you'll find lots of inspiration within these pages, and if you'd like to see more, I invite you to explore **picturebookmakers.com**.

Sam McCullen | dPICTUS

Blexbolex 8

Eva Lindström 20

Shaun Tan 30

Beatrice Alemagna 40

Chris Haughton 52

Kitty Crowther 64

Jon Klassen 76

Suzy Lee 90

Bernardo P. Carvalho 100

Isol 114

Manuel Marsol 124

Johanna Schaible 138

ILLUSTRATION BY JOHANNA SCHAIBLE

Blexbolex

FRANCE

Blexbolex (Bernard Granger) is an award-winning French illustrator who lives in Berlin. His books have been published all over the world, and he's widely revered for his experimental approach to printmaking and book production. Blexbolex won the 'Best Book Design from All Over the World' award at the Leipzig Book Fair.

In this chapter, Blexbolex talks about the creation of *Romance (Ballad)*. This incredible picturebook was originally published in French by Albin Michel Jeunesse, and has been translated into numerous languages including English, Spanish, Italian, Polish and German.

Blexbolex: *Ballad* comes after *People* (Albin Michel, 2008) and *Seasons* (Albin Michel, 2009) and was expected to be a picturebook of stories. I had to keep the same structure of the page – a word / an image – so it would fit within the trilogy.

When I started this project at the end of 2009, I had no idea about how to organise it. I had desires and atmospheres in my head but nothing really concrete. Little by little, it became clear that the pictures in the book must by themselves – progressively and step by step – be embedded in a narrative continuity and form a kind of story.

The pages of the book contain, for the most part, quotes from all kinds of stories or visual or literary quotations – some well-known, others less so.

The trigger for the form was firstly my stay with a group of artists working on comics in an unconventional way: OuBaPo. One of the exercises captured my imagination. It involved inserting one square of a comic strip between two existing squares, thereby diverting the narrative ellipsis towards another one. Then a meeting with a group of children gave me the real key to the book. They were playing a game where whatever path they took, they always got to arrive home. That put me on the path of rhymes, cumulative songs, old folk songs and on the somehow musical structure of the book.

It also reminded me in a funny way of my own childhood memories – when I came home from school, of course. Seeing that the book was going in the direction of storytelling, I also read *Morphology of the Folktale* by Vladimir Propp to make sure I didn't forget the milestones of the story genre.

cola
apple juice
the feast,

the bandits,

IV N7

Personnages magiques :

3 I École, chemin, maison

V 33

5 II École, Rue, chemin, forêt, maison

9 III École, Rue, Place, chemin, (...), forêt, (...), maison.

17 IV École, (...), Rue, (...), Place, Pont, Chemin, (...), Forêt, (...), Maison

33 V

65 VI de VI au pont commence à douter de V — avion canoë cascade nénuphars (personnage fantastique

129 VII Reflets — nuit voie lactée — Retour au réel — puis très T à T : portail, maison, fin

VI 65 Toute la séquence est nocturne — le fleuve — voyage cosmique — retour sur terre → certaines images des séquences précédentes sont donc célestes en VII, oniriques

Pont, Bataille, ~~...~~, reflets

T III IV V IV III ~~VI~~

: Bataille est suivi de Reflets donc B = VI et R = VII puisque R est la résolution finale de la Proposition.

~~I II~~

I	I	I	I	I	I	I	École
II	II	II	II	II	II		rue
III	III	III	III	III			Place
IV	IV	IV	IV				Magasin
V	V	V					Vitrine
VI	VI						
VII							

École

Trans-séquence ~~Séquence~~ entière et résolue :

É	Ru	Pl	P	F	B	R
I	II	III	IV	V	VI	VII

On the left is one of my hundreds of pages of notes. Here, I'm still rather far from the final book, testing how the form could work with the elements and means. Hours and hours of calculations.

The first six parts of the book were rather improvised, but it then became so complicated that I needed to do some kind of a storyboard. You can see an example above.

I faced difficulties of all kinds throughout the making of the book. The constraints were huge and the difficulty to remain consistent until the end progressively increased. I can't state all the difficulties I faced, but some were technical and related to the narrative (there are sequences that I fully started, rewrote and redesigned, even though the book was already half done), and some were related to time and money. I initially tried to finance the book alone by accepting all the illustration work possible – but in doing so, I had no more time for the book. I felt like I was trapped under a spell, where each attempt to make the book moved the possibility of its completion even further away.

What put an end to this vicious circle was the allocation of a creativity grant from the National Book Centre (CNL), which allowed me to work with the necessary continuity. I'm very grateful to them.

My publisher at Albin Michel also provided me with constant support from beginning to end. We kept in touch by email and sometimes she had to read thousands of explanations, the poor thing! I'm kidding. Everyone at Albin Michel was great, really.

Over all this time, my drawing was changing, so I had to stop making new pages in order to redo the older ones. Here you can see the oldest versions of some of the scenes and characters along with the final work. The images for the book are purely digital; only three backgrounds on paper (two with pencil and one with ink wash painting) were scanned in to allow me to add substance to the shapes drawn on the computer. I had to redo the bridge scene for technical reasons, and could never catch the light and atmosphere again. As revenge, I printed the old picture as a small poster – a three-colour silkscreen.

✓ this one

le pont,

the bridge,

l'étranger,

the stranger,

les bandits,

the bandits,

la sorcière,

the witch,

The witch is one of the main characters in the book. Her aim is to replace the small world that is being built page after page with her own. And she really wants it! If the spells she casts only affected the other characters or objects, but not the words, it seemed to me that this would have less impact on the imagination of the readers. The witch is the true antagonist and she wants to make the book disappear in order to take control, so it seemed logical to me that when she reaches the peak of her power, she can remove the things that were referenced earlier. Her victory may seem almost complete at this point. But despite her power, she only manages to win half the world, so it still has a chance to become itself again. I think this creates suspense and an expectation in this sense.

One of the consequences of this approach is that the gap between the words and images becomes very open. The child reader can have fun remembering the missing words, or perhaps making up their own or questioning them. They can play with their memory or imagination and participate in the story, as I invite them to do.

They can become the author too.

the adventure,

the ,

Eva Lindström

SWEDEN

Eva Lindström studied at Västerås Art School and Konstfack in Stockholm, and has since created a long list of highly acclaimed picturebooks. For her contribution to children's literature, Eva was nominated for the Hans Christian Andersen Award and the Nordic Council Children and Young People's Literature Prize.

In this chapter, Eva talks about her process and the creation of her charming and beautifully illustrated picturebook *Alla går iväg (Everyone Walks Away)*. This understated tale of friendship and loneliness was originally published by Alfabeta in Sweden.

Eva: This is how the story goes: Three characters walk away. One character is left all alone. Then this character walks away too. At the end, the three characters appear again and the lonely one invites them to a tea party.

The story is rather quiet and emotional and it ends in an open way. The reader will be able to finish the book herself, or accept that it ends with a question.

I always start with just a fragment of an idea when I begin working on a book. A state of mind, a diffuse idea, a feeling of something that can turn into a story. And then, the more I write and rewrite, the clearer it gets, or it gets unclear in an interesting way.

All of the pictures are in my head while writing. The colours, the personalities, the landscapes... Everything is there, pointing out a possible way to tell a specific story. And the stories often circle around subjects, such as lost things, lost people, friendship and no friendship, longing... I really try to tell stories about other things too, but I seldom succeed.

This time, it happened to be a story about how one character is sad because he thinks that 'everyone' is walking away. His name is Frank, and the ones who walk are Palle, Titti and Milan.

Why do they walk away? Does Frank enjoy being an outsider? Is Frank the one who is leaving? Is everyone walking away?

I don't ask these questions while working on the book. It is when the book is ready that I first start to wonder: What is happening? Who does what? A good thing for me is to not know everything.

First there is the text, and then the pictures.

I start to paint and everything changes; a new story is told without words. And the best part of the whole thing is when I work with the words and pictures together. I rearrange the text (it is not allowed to say too much), cut most of it, write new pieces. And as the text changes, I paint another room, other trees, other faces.

I want there to be a space in both the words and pictures: small gaps where the reader can walk around. It is important that the text is not a fence.

If I am lucky, a certain humour can appear when the words meet the pictures in an unexpected way.

In this book, as with some of my others, I have mixed people and animals. Frank has a rather long nose and Milan has a longer one. The other two seem to be ordinary people. One reason for me to mix the species is because I feel that the pictures become interesting. Different kinds of bodies and faces make the pictures attractive and I have fun while drawing them. Another reason might be that this animal/human mix moves the story to a place outside the everyday world.

It is hard to clearly explain all the decisions that are made while working on a book. I think that the work itself, how it proceeds, makes things happen. Along the way I see options; the story has suggestions. I can follow these suggestions, and one thing opens up to something else.

Some years ago, I never did any sketches for my books. Now I do. Not always, but sometimes, and I am beginning to see the point in doing them. I don't make them detailed – only very simple sketches that show in a vague way how things might be.

My working materials are watercolour, gouache and graphite. I paint on an Arches paper (300g, satin). I like it very much when transparent watercolour meets thick gouache, and I also like graphite contours – and spaces covered with graphite. This is how I do it right now; I might change my approach soon.

A good thing with gouache is that it helps me to cover my mistakes. It is easy to paint something else on top of something that went totally wrong (I don't use a computer). The resulting composition can be a surprise. The picture can take a new direction, as if I was not involved in the decision. A dark tree hides something and the picture gets a new balance.

Here are some badly painted hares. The picture is from a book called *We Are Friends* (Alfabeta, 2014). Some of these trees and stumps would not exist if it were not for the 'hare failures'.

Han rör då och då
och gråter lite mer
när det verkar bli
för tjockt.
Det ska inte vara för tjockt
men det ska inte
vara för löst heller
marmelad

It is always a step in the right direction to do something that I am disgruntled with.

Coincidences, accidents and failures are my best friends.

And here is Frank. He is leaving his room now. The story will soon end. He has been crying in a pan. He added 4 dl of sugar. He has cooked and stirred for hours.

The marmalade is ready to eat.

He will now invite the others for tea.

Shaun Tan

AUSTRALIA

Shaun Tan grew up in Perth. As well as writing and illustrating world-renowned books, he's worked as a concept artist for animated films such as Pixar's WALL-E, and he directed the Academy Award-winning short film *The Lost Thing* with Passion Pictures Australia. In 2011, Shaun received the Astrid Lindgren Memorial Award.

In this chapter, Shaun talks about the creation of *Rules of Summer* and he gives a fascinating insight into his working process. This wonderfully surreal picturebook was originally published by Hachette Australia in 2013 and has been translated into over twenty languages.

Shaun: *Rules of Summer* is a picturebook that had a very long gestation; I'd been thinking about it for a decade or so, mainly trying to figure out just what the story could be.

I routinely draw lots of little vignettes in small sketchbooks, like loose bones in search of some connective tissue that might lead to a narrative, and in this case that narrative proved very hard to find. I just had lots of scenes of two characters, modelled more or less on myself and my older brother as kids, getting caught in all manner of odd situations. Eventually it occurred to me to forget about story altogether – why not? In fact, one thing I love about picturebooks is an ability to depart from linear narrative, and particularly from explanation. I think readers appreciate that too, the ability to freely imagine what is going on in each picture.

Just to give you an idea of what I mean, I'll show you a couple of consecutive images with very spare text. 'Never leave a red sock on the clothes-line' is a kind of self-contained little story of its own, albeit very enigmatic. [1]

Turning the page finds us in another place altogether, with the cautionary line, 'Never eat the last olive at a party'. [2]

For me this kind of structure, or lack thereof, actually reminds me of childhood, the memory of which can feel quite jumbled and discontinuous.

At the same time, there's a sort of emotional connectivity under the surface (always the same two boys with a particular power relationship), and that's always been my main interest: how we identify ourselves, and our values and desires, within a changing and unexpected world.

But rather than talk too much about overall themes, I thought it would be more interesting to focus on a single illustration, and look at some progressive ideas and sketches.

I think I'm quite a slow illustrator, and have a habit of drawing the same images over and over again, and this is a good place to show a little of this working style.

First the concept, which usually comes to me as quite a vague mental picture. In this case, centred on the relationship between a person and a gang of oddball creatures, something along the lines of a much earlier illustration from my book, *Tales from Outer Suburbia*. [3]

The creature with a single big eye in particular tends to recur throughout my work, as do scenes of humans trying to relate to non-humans, as you can see in a pencil drawing some years later. [4]

It's a sort of evolutionary step towards *Rules of Summer* (at the time just called 'summer project' in my filing cabinet) in which the focus has shifted to a relationship between two human characters, possibly a brother and sister. In the drawing below, one of them is enjoying a backyard birthday party while the other is left out, but we don't quite know the reason. Maybe he wasn't invited, or forgot to bring a gift, or shy, we just don't know.

And in another similar scene sketched with a biro, for a possible graphic novel, I plotted out eighty pages before deciding it didn't feel quite right. [5] Here the two characters, now both boys, are having an argument over a boundary line, which leads to a fight. The creatures are a gang of dismayed onlookers, the idea being that they represent a deeper emotional knowledge beneath all the bickering. I still like these scenes very much, but unfortunately I could not wrangle a sustained tale out

[3]

[4]

RUINS OF DETROIT
[5]
[6]
[7]
BUDGIES WON'T CARRY YOU UNLESS YOU ASK
- WRECKS.
NEVER LEAVE A RED SOCK ON THE LINE
SUMMER
LOOK!
SOME ARE GOOD AT MAKING FRIENDS
NEVER TURN UP EMPTY HANDED
SOME RELIGIONS ONLY LAST FOR A SINGLE AFTERNOON
THE BEST FISHING IS IN NEW YORK CITY

of them, and it all felt a bit overwrought. So then I thought, let's forget about storylines or sequencing, and just see how different ideas look when shuffled together randomly. [6] Most of these sketchy vignettes fell by the wayside, but not without establishing a kind of tone or loose scaffolding. One idea that survived was, again, this 'creature-gang' scene (with the caption: 'some are good at making friends'). I liked it because it reminded me of certain real childhood experiences. I elaborated the creature-gang doodle, where you can see a group of several creatures marching along in the foreground, led by a boy who is waving to another boy in the background, who is reading a book beside a big creature on a hill. [7]

The concept has something to do with competition, pride and envy: one kid is demonstrating how good he is at making lots of friends – literally, since all the creatures are big robots – while the other is being left behind. Notably, a sort of boundary line is still present, defined by a road.

I sketched the scene again, but with the emotional tone adjusted. [8]

The boy on the hill is building the one-eyed creature, and is far from finished. The other, now more defined as an older brother, is essentially ignoring the younger and regarding his watch, his body language radiating impatience. The working caption was simply: 'don't be late'. I liked this variation because the relationship between the characters now felt slightly autobiographical. I identify with the younger incompetent one!

So once I think the concept sketch is working, I'll refine my drawings on a larger piece of paper. [9]

Often what I do is scan and enlarge the concept sketch, and trace over it on a lightbox to get the basic composition, and then refine each element.

My attention here is mainly on composition and character, how the viewer's eye moves through an image, and what emotional resonances can be conveyed – as well as getting the balance of weirdness and familiarity just right, with not too much of either.

You want to invite the reader through the door without telling them where they are.

[8]

[9]

[10]

Next I'll create a small colour sketch using acrylic paint and pastel crayons, thinking about light, atmosphere as well as the way that colour can draw attention to certain details, such as the one-eyed creature on the hill. [10]

I wanted the mood of the painting to be delightful, partly because it's a fun scene, but also to contrast with a darker tension between the brothers. I always enjoy that kind of ambiguous mood.

Now happy with the composition, I began working on a final painting with pastel crayons on a large bit of unprimed canvas, enjoying the softness and immediacy of this medium. [11] While this painting is fine on its own, the feeling wasn't quite right for the book overall, perhaps a little too dark or static, the details a bit fussy.

I started over again, this time working in oils, using mainly a palette knife to achieve a slightly less controlled texture, and hoped this might liven up the scene.

The final oil painting is 30 x 34 inches, executed over several stages and taking about four to

[11]

five working days. [12] The main difference is a brighter colour, closer to the original colour sketch, but you'll also notice some elements changed (a fish and bird removed, some buildings added). I don't think this is necessarily a better painting, but it's better for this moment in the book, which needed to feel sunny and bright. One advantage of oil paint is that it's easy to revise, unlike pastels. That's important when working on a series, as sometimes I need to go back and make little changes, anything from a character's face to an overall varnish of colour. While I can edit digitally, I prefer to get things right by hand as much as possible.

The final text accompanying the image is small and understated on the facing page: 'Never be late for a parade'. It adds a little context without overinterpreting the painting, and the word 'Never' ended up as a connecting thread between all pictures, and ultimately informed the title, *Rules of Summer*.

I will often rewrite the text multiple times as the last part of a book project, in part because it's far easier to change than the paintings!

[12]

So that's an example of one piece of a larger puzzle, and I always feel that the unseen evolution of an idea is as interesting as the final result. After all, that's the thing that gets me hooked as a creator, having a sense that something is bubbling its way to the surface, and really just wanting to see what it looks like!

The complete work is often slightly surprising: oh, so that's what it looks like.

Nothing to do but go back to the sketchbook and move on to the next one...

Beatrice Alemagna

ITALY

Beatrice Alemagna, who grew up in Bologna and now lives in Paris, has created over thirty books which have been published around the world. Her many accolades include the Premio Andersen Award, a BolognaRagazzi Mention, five White Ravens Awards, and three Baobab Prizes for the most innovative books for children.

In this chapter, Beatrice talks about the creation of her stunning picturebook *Le Merveilleux Dodu-Velu-Petit (The Wonderful Fluffy Little Squishy)*. She also shares some invaluable insights into her approach to storytelling and picturebook making.

Beatrice: I'm self-taught. I never attended a school of illustration, and everything I've learnt has been through making children's books. I learnt by experimenting on my own, at my table.

I've been making books for over fifteen years and each time feels like the first time.

Le Merveilleux Dodu-Velu-Petit (The Wonderful Fluffy Little Squishy) is a book that required six years of reflection and two years of solid work.

Since I was little, I've been fascinated by an episode of *Pippi Longstocking* in which she decided to look for 'Spunk', a word she invented and something that doesn't exist at that time. It's always stayed with me – the idea that in the end, you always find those things that don't exist. And I convinced myself that this would require a long search in the shops.

This book is partly a homage to Pippi and the fascination I experienced when I was little: entering a shop full of things that were waiting to be discovered.

The most difficult thing that I'd wanted to convey from the beginning was a sense of lightness. Over the last few years, I've started to take lightness very seriously – not lightly, as I did before.

For me, lightness has become the place where serious things come together. Upon reflection, I understood that lightness might elude us because of its subtlety. It's not banal, and can in fact become the peak of tension in seriousness. The light discovery of something unique (like in Eddie's adventure) summarises the idea of childhood that I wanted to convey in this book.

Childhood as a moment of glory.

The whole book stems from the character of Dodu. One day, out of nowhere, I drew this kind of electrified dog and I instantly felt the need to tell its story.

Often the characters themselves call out to us, and for me it's nearly always like this. At first, this book was destined for Japanese readers. I started my very first drawing six or seven years before the book was finished. But the story was very different back then. [p.46] The main character and the search in the shops were already there, but the little girl didn't have a character yet, and the adventures Eddie lives through today didn't exist.

I spent years taking photos of the most beautiful shop windows during my trips around the world. My writing and all this research were left in my drawer for nearly six years: the necessary time for it to mature and come to life.

I wrote and rewrote my story at least ten times, asking myself how I could actually manage to tell what I wanted to through an adventure. A simple and classic adventure, in literary terms.

I'd never written a real adventure before and it turned out to be a hard task.

With this in mind, *Le Merveilleux Dodu-Velu-Petit* was very new for me. But inside lie the core themes of nearly all of my books: travel, departure, the search for something, and accepting oneself. I think, deep down, I always want to tell the same story: a fragile being that finds great strength within himself.

My drawings required dozens of attempts as well. When I draw, I'm always looking for something. I keep going until I find something that tells me: yes, you're on the right track; this really couldn't be any other way.

In order to tell this story with a 'light language', I wanted some of the main factors of fragility to play a part. Children are extremely fragile and Dodu is an abandoned, vulnerable being.

I wanted to talk about care, about every form of attention, research, and love (through the love for her mum, the little girl discovers the love for

herself and her friends, who help her and advise her, offering her care and love).

I also tried to convey lightness in a visual way: snow, birds, steaming tea, gushing water, ruffled hair, Eddie running. I wanted all this lightness to tell the story of the immense and fundamental power of fantasy. And the character of Dodu, with his bold colours and peculiar face, symbolises exactly this power.

I grew up in Italy with the popular traditions of Gianni Rodari, Luigi Malerba, Collodi, De Amicis... Children have always been connected, as in my childhood, with society and its problems. And so are all the characters in my books: beings in need.

Thanks to my love of foreign cultures (for example, English nonsense, Japanese animism, German surrealism, and the magic of Russian and Scandinavian fairy tales), I always try to explore new worlds and new visual languages.

It's absolutely impossible to identify myself with something precise, because I want to explore, change and evolve – even at the risk of letting my readers down. My books always emerge from a million doubts, reflections and redrafts. Nothing is clear to me while I'm making a book, but everything flows naturally in my head. The hardest thing is trying to reach it. I would like to say that I write books in the same way as I see or think. But this isn't true. While drawing is perfectly natural to me, creating a book with a narrative pace to be respected is a laborious and sometimes painful process. But at the end of the book, the suffering always makes way for immense happiness.

I love mixtures and hybrids. I love avoiding walls or barriers, not worrying about age limits, time limits, precise aesthetic rules, pre-established conventions. All of this comes from a huge trust in myself. I always work with something from within, which is strong and expresses itself very clearly and intensely.

Lastly, I love paradoxes: my books often have big formats (I don't like feeling constrained by the page), but they often talk about small things. I love discovering minuscule things in nature, in people's faces, in the emotions I feel. Small things, like fragile things, are what move me the most.

LE MERVEILLEUX DODU-VELU-PETIT. Copyright © 2014 Albin Michel Jeunesse. Reproduced by permission of the publisher, Albin Michel, Paris, France. For a list of the different language editions, see Beatrice's post on picturebookmakers.com.

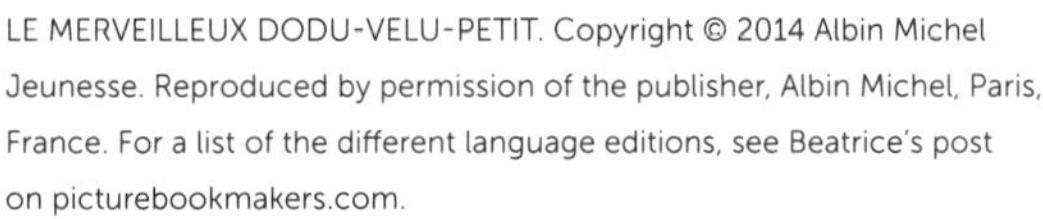

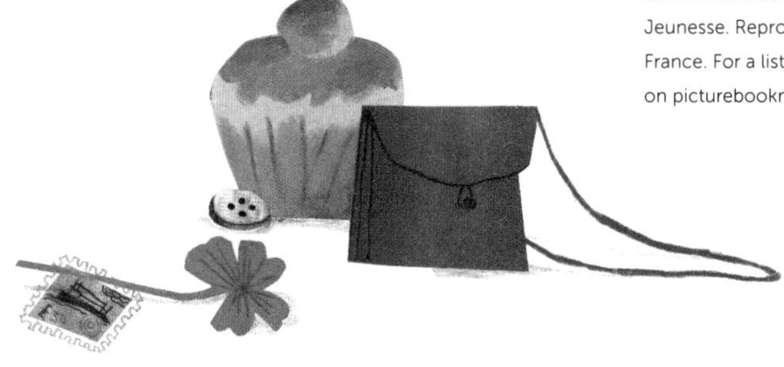

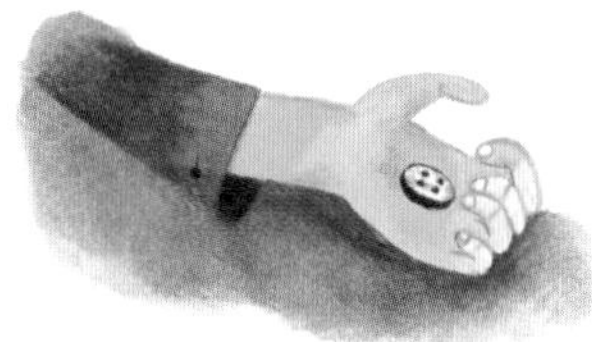

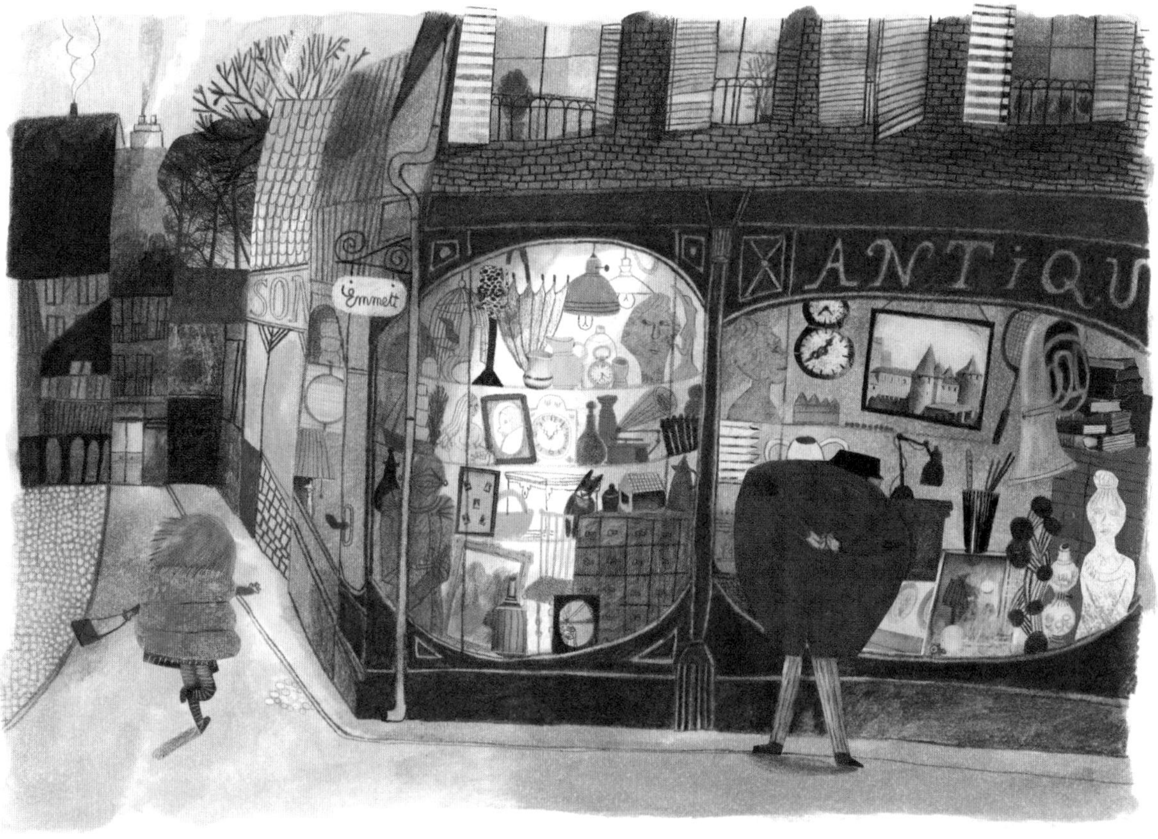

AU CH
ANIMAUX
ÉCOLE
MODE
BROSSES
Bar
PAPETERIE

AGE
OUETS
Salon de Coiffure
BARBIER

Chris Haughton

IRELAND

Chris Haughton's first picturebook *A Bit Lost* has been translated into around thirty languages and has won many international awards, including the Premio Andersen Award. Chris co-founded the fair trade social business NODE, and he was listed in Time Magazine's 'Design 100' for his work with the fair trade company People Tree. Born in Dublin, Chris now lives and works in London.

In this chapter, Chris talks about the creation of his bold and inventive picturebook *Shh! We Have a Plan*. Originally published in the UK by Walker Books, the book has been translated into numerous languages including Spanish, Japanese and Swedish.

Chris: As an illustrator, it's been drilled into me that I need to simplify everything to communicate something elemental – so I try to find the very essence of a story and strip everything else back.

One of the things I've been trying with my books is to tell stories as much as possible through images rather than through words. If the story can be read without language, it should have the ability to be understood by the very young. I'd like to think all my books are told in a way that someone without language could understand, but I think this book could be the most visual. It certainly has the least text. In fact, the total word count is a hundred and three, and ten of those words are "shh", which I'm not sure is a word, but I counted it anyway.

I started sketching out ideas thinking there must be some way of making a chase / catch type book. It was sparked by seeing an incredibly inspiring show at the Edinburgh Fringe by Mr. Bunk called Swamp Juice. It brought me around to thinking of the Road Runner cartoons where there are elaborate plans which could work well visually. Quite suddenly, three goon-type characters trying to trap a bird popped into my head – and I thought it would be great if they each had a different plan.

What I liked the best was there could be a drawn-out pantomime effect (similar to *A Bit Lost* and *Oh No, George!*) with an anticipatory page-turn between "ready, steady" – where the three position themselves to catch the bird – and "GO!"... where of course, they miss.

Finding the ending was easy as I had sort of come up with it in the beginning! The really tricky part was fitting it into the story...

Shh!

WE HAVE A PLAN

CHRIS HAUGHTON

ready one

ready two
ready three ...

I originally had three other 'good' characters who were feeding the birds – but it seemed abrupt to introduce them midway. It was best to have a character with the answer the whole way through.

The book seemed a little clunky and wordy when mocked up with four or five characters on every page, so together with my art director, Deirdre, we hit on the idea of a conversation happening across the page.

There was lots of comic potential with this. It makes use of repetition, where each character repeats the same thing, over and over again. It's predictable, but it also has a pantomime effect and is great for doing silly voices.

tip-toe
slowly
tip-toe
slowly
now stop
shh!

For my first two books, I'm always asked if I used paper cut, as they look quite like it – but in fact I didn't use paper cut at all when creating the artwork. It was all pencil and digital. For this book though, because it had five characters on each page, it needed some sort of drastic simplification for it to be read clearly. Not only that, but I was keen for the conversations to read across the page, matching each line with the action of the character. There was so much shifting of compositions around on the pages that it became clear the best way to compose each page was by collage. In fact, it made perfect sense to create a mainly silhouette image from paper cut – and the design of the birds benefitted from it too.

I was keen that that the bird seemed somehow from another world – brightly coloured, abstracted and removed from the world of the characters. It focuses all our attention on the relatively tiny bird on the page, leads the reader through the pages of the book, and gives a punch of colour at the end.

My other books are very colourful, so it was quite satisfying to try to work almost entirely in silhouette for this one. In fact, there were a lot of really interesting experiments with the colour. Usually, full colour printing is in CMYK, but the whole of this book is printed in only CMK (blue, magenta and black), and the only yellow that appears in the book is in the colour of the birds. It was our hope that with this approach, the bird would stand out completely from the rest of the book.

I am hugely indebted to my art director and editors, Deirdre McDermott and David Lloyd for all their feedback and help on this book. It improved immeasurably with their help and I consider myself very lucky to be working with them.

 For a list of the different language editions, see Chris's post on picturebookmakers.com.

Kitty Crowther

BELGIUM

Kitty Crowther, who is half English and half Swedish, was born in Brussels, and now lives and works in Wallonia in Belgium. She's written and illustrated around forty books which have been translated into over twenty languages. In 2010, Kitty received the Astrid Lindgren Memorial Award.

In this chapter, Kitty talks about the creation of *Mère Méduse (Mother Medusa)*, and she shares some enchanting sketches and illustrations. This striking picturebook about the maternal bond was originally published in French by Pastel–l'école des loisirs.

Kitty: It was the fiftieth anniversary of l'école des loisirs in 2015. I used to read those books as a child and loved them over and over. I've now been working with Pastel (the Belgian imprint of l'école des loisirs) for almost thirty years. One of my more recent picturebooks with Pastel is called *Mère Méduse*. To translate the title into English, I would say 'Mother Medusa' and not 'Mother Jellyfish'. Even though medusa and jellyfish are connected. For me, Mother Medusa is a descendant of Medusa from Greek mythology. I'll come back to that.

The English name jellyfish has been used since 1796, although the term medusa was coined a short time before this by Linnaeus (more famous as Linné, the Swedish botanist. He was so famous that you could just refer to him as L). The Swedish author August Strindberg wrote: 'Linnaeus was in reality a poet who happened to become a naturalist'. To keep it short, Linnaeus classified and named all the living things, and he gave jellyfish the name medusa because their tentacles made him think of the hair of Medusa, one of the three Gorgons from Greek mythology.

I remember speaking about the future with my eldest son Theodore, back when he was 17 (he's in his 20s now). I was trying to find out what he wanted to do when he was older. For fun, he asked me the same question. I smiled, and at first I said entomologist (someone who studies insects), but after several arguments, we opted for biologist.

I thought about how I love every living thing. I have a huge weakness for birds, flowers, stones. And insects, of course.

So I'm sorry to invade your space with jellyfish. And science notions. But I like to talk about them.

I find jellyfish amazing.

There's as much saline density in the body of a jellyfish as there is in the sea. This is why they can stay so still. It's as if they are on hold. I like to watch them swim slowly. I tell myself that they've been in the oceans for 650 million years; I don't even understand this length of time.

It's as if they are guards. I'm really not surprised that they play an important ecological role. There's even talk of a species that's immortal.

When I was a little girl, I watched jellyfish in fascination (those that were stranded on the beach), and I tried to put them back in the water. Of course I got stung. But whatever.

A fascinating beauty to keep at a distance. Just like the character in my book *Mother Medusa*, who holds the world at a distance. It's as if she's locked up in her own hair. Only her daughter can approach her. So much hair she cannot untangle it.

Back to the story. I won this amazing prize in 2010 (the Astrid Lindgren Memorial Award) and I've travelled all over the world (to my delight), but sometimes it was too much. I didn't have the time to write or draw. I also need time to do nothing. And a very particular kind of listening: to hear what wants to return. I very often say that it's not the author that chooses the story, but the story that chooses you.

Sometimes I'm so happy to have finished a book. Then nothing is planned... but it doesn't last for long, like apnea, between inhaling and exhaling. And I wonder what will happen this time.

In 2012, I had a wonderful expo in Moulins, France. Five rooms in the Musée de l'Illustration Jeunesse. I made a big drawing with a hundred characters. They printed it very large and mounted it on the wall so that the children could colour it in. [p.68] It was so nice to be 'in it' rather than looking at it on a sheet of paper. And in this myriad of characters, a very strange woman appeared next to a very nice little girl. They've come back again since then, on a poster. Increasingly present.

Drawing hair is fascinating. I have total admiration for a book called *Letterdromen met Do* by Harriet van Reek. I love how the hair is presented. Sometimes resembling algae. Not far from a Japanese universe. There are lots of things to say about it. The thread, the link, the spider, and so on. I won't get into a psychoanalysis; I'll leave that to you.

The mythological character Medusa touches me deeply. Do you know her story? Here's one version: It is said that Medusa was extremely beautiful. So beautiful that Poseidon took her and raped her in the temple of Athena (daughter of Zeus, a virgin and a great warrior). Furiously, Athena metamorphosed Medusa along with her two immortal sisters (Euryale and Stheno). Her hair became snakes and her eyes dilated and petrified all who crossed her... Perseus beheaded her (I'll let you discover the epic), and from her sliced neck, Chrysaor (who had a golden sword) and Pegasus (yes, yes, the flying horse) were born. My Medusa is in line with Chrysaor.

The power of the woman, the power of the look (a fatal woman), the fear of castration, the intimate relationship with the monstrous and the existence of prehistoric matriarchal societies. All of this in one woman!

I juggle with ancient symbols and mythical references. All powerful. Remember, I do not choose.

I thought of these very rebellious women, just like punks. I wondered how one can come into the world and have a mother like that. A little like Calamity Jane (read the beautiful book *Calamity Jane's Letters to Her Daughter*, even though the authenticity of the letters is disputed).

Female borderline. Who loves wrongly, but loves dearly. Being a little sweet one. Deeply sweet. She loves her mother, that's for sure. But she would love to join others who are just like her.

Through travelling, the story developed in my mind. And I didn't stop feeding it. Thinking about it. Seeing the magical bonds within it.

I struggled to begin the story. Usually, it's obvious. But Medusa was very difficult to tame. I wanted to go in a certain direction – make her a bit witch-like, like a caricature, or a little like Tove Jansson – but each time it was a total rejection.

During the creation of this book, I spent some time in Sweden (my mother is Swedish). I love all the flat rocks that live in the water there. They look like they've been polished by the ice and wind...

I try to make timeless stories. No phone, no television. Just people, the sky, the ground and everything that grows, walks and flies.

I have another fascination: iridescent colour. Like rainbows or like the oil remaining on the surface of the water. A little gross, but so beautiful to watch. Like nacre.

 For a list of the different language editions, see Kitty's post on picturebookmakers.com.

Jon Klassen

CANADA

Jon Klassen grew up in Niagara Falls and now lives in Los Angeles. After working as an illustrator on animated feature films, music videos and editorial pieces, he debuted as a picturebook artist with *I Want My Hat Back*. Jon has since received many awards for his work, including the Caldecott and Kate Greenaway Medals.

In this chapter, Jon talks about his *Hat Trilogy*. These three outstanding picturebooks have together sold over two million copies, spent several years on the New York Times bestseller list, and have been translated into more than thirty languages.

Jon: I'm going to talk about making these three books: *I Want My Hat Back*, *This Is Not My Hat* and *We Found A Hat*.

I've illustrated other books, but these were the first books I wrote, so I'll talk more about the writing side than the illustrating.

When I was getting more into making books full-time, it became clear pretty quickly that I needed to start writing my own if it was going to be a viable thing, but I had a problem in that I didn't like drawing characters. I like drawing scenery and inanimate objects and I especially liked it back then. The challenge of making a piece where the subject wasn't a living thing was really fun, and I liked how quiet the effect was.

Drawing characters always seemed like cheating, somehow. Like it was an easy way to get the audience's attention and focus. I like a story that allows the viewer to wander around a little bit and find it on their own. I think my distaste for drawing characters owes partially to sensibility and partially to me just being scared of making them up. Making up a character always seemed kind of impossible.

Around this same time I was asked to make some greeting cards for a company called Red Cap Cards. I sent them some sketches of chairs and inanimate objects and they wrote back asking if I might try my hand at something a little more engaging, like some characters. I argued that I didn't really do that, but they were (and are) friends and they were comfortable enough to come back and ask again. What I eventually sent them was a series of animals wearing birthday hats and holding balloons, but their faces and

poses made them look, to me, like they had no idea what a birthday was and didn't really care. I was excited by this approach. It made me laugh, and it got me off the hook. I wasn't creating a character when I drew them; I was borrowing them for a minute to put them on this card, like a photographer who gets someone to pose for them and this is the best they could get.

I also liked the bear that appeared on one of the cards. Even though he was completely still and emotionless, he looked like potentially a threat. He was a bear, after all. I thought that since I had broken the seal on drawing a character I could maybe use him in a book. I thought of maybe taking his hat away and then calling the book *I Want My Hat Back*.

It was a while between deciding on that idea and figuring out how to write it. For a long time I had it written with narration. It sounded like this:

A bear has lost his hat.
"Where is my hat?" he said.

I hated it. I didn't really know what I wanted the narration to do, what it was adding, and I had no real story anyway. I can't remember what prompted it, but one night I thought of doing the whole thing only in dialogue instead, without narration, and using colours to show who was talking so I wouldn't even have to name anybody.

The idea of just doing it in dialogue with the pictures next to them suggested that one of them might be lying, and we could show the audience that they were lying.

After that, the story came very quickly and organically.

The illustrations were kept really simple. I always liked picturebooks that were very clean, but I was afraid to do them too clean for someone else's text for fear it would look lazy. For my own books it was really fun.

Also, when you leave out a lot, your roughs come out pretty close to the final.

The book was written in very stiff language. It was stiff because I was nervous about writing a book, and I liked the idea that these characters were not very good at speaking their lines, so they came out stiff and they kept looking at the camera / audience instead of at each other like they should be when two characters are speaking to each other.

They seemed baffled to be in a book, as I was baffled to be making one.

The process of making this book ended up loosely being the process for making the two books that followed it: Choosing a simple (and hopefully visual) problem – in this case a bear who wants to be wearing his hat again – then deciding how it will be told – in this case with dialogue between characters – and letting that second decision suggest the story itself.

After *I Want My Hat Back* was finished, I wanted to try other books using the same characters and location. I'd enjoyed the atmosphere of the book, however minimal it is. Along the highways in Ontario, Canada where I'm from there are these patches of low forest that grow when you travel north a little ways. The trees don't get higher than six feet or so and they grow out of tall grasses and scrubby bushes. I always pictured these animals living somewhere like that, heads poking out of the plants, and I liked hanging out there and thinking about them.

I thought maybe there could be a book about the deer. He was the only one in the first book who took any real interest in the bear's problem, and he looked to me physically sympathetic. Kind of hunched shoulders and thin and frail.

I tried a few versions of books about him. The first story was about the deer saying he liked to be alone at night (he doesn't) and going around waking up other animals to see if they shared this feeling. The only idea in this book that I liked was that he goes to wake up the turtle, but the turtle is asleep and in his sleep describes a dream where he is floating off into the stars. It didn't really fit into the story, but it was a nice little aside.

The second story was about the deer trying to trade a stick that he found for other objects that the animals have now acquired. Eventually, the mole creature from *I Want My Hat Back* appears and shows him how to light the stick on fire, but that goes nowhere good.

After a few of these deer stories I started to realise that I was just copying the format of the first book and it wasn't coming as naturally. My art director at Candlewick, knowing I didn't like what I was getting out of this strategy, suggested I "go somewhere else" completely with the setting and characters. So I thought of doing a story with light characters on a dark background, and that suggested being deep underwater, so it might be about fish.

The first fish story really didn't concern a hat at all. It was called *Ten Bad Fish* and it was kind of a western about a gang of fish that ride into town and terrorise successively bigger and bigger fish

until they wake up an especially big one and turn around and head back, but are now being eaten one by one from behind until there is only one left, and the book ends without showing if the last one gets eaten or not. It was a dark book, and again it didn't really have anybody very redeeming in it. You didn't like the gang, and you didn't really like the big fish either, so there was nobody to root for.

My editor asked if I could lighten it up at all, and I realised my favourite part of the story was the very end, when there was one little gang member fish left with a big fish somewhere off the page behind him, wondering if he would be spared.

The structure of *This Is Not My Hat* came from two very well-known stories about feeling guilty.

The first is *The Tell-Tale Heart* by Edgar Allan Poe. My favourite stories of his are his unreliable narrator ones; he always knew just how to remind you what it felt like to be in big trouble but trying to talk yourself out of feeling bad about it. The idea of a character talking to you about how and why he committed the crime when you felt like all the while you were walking him to the gallows is a really good fit for a picturebook because you can show that walk (or swim, in this case), and contrast it with what he's saying in the text.

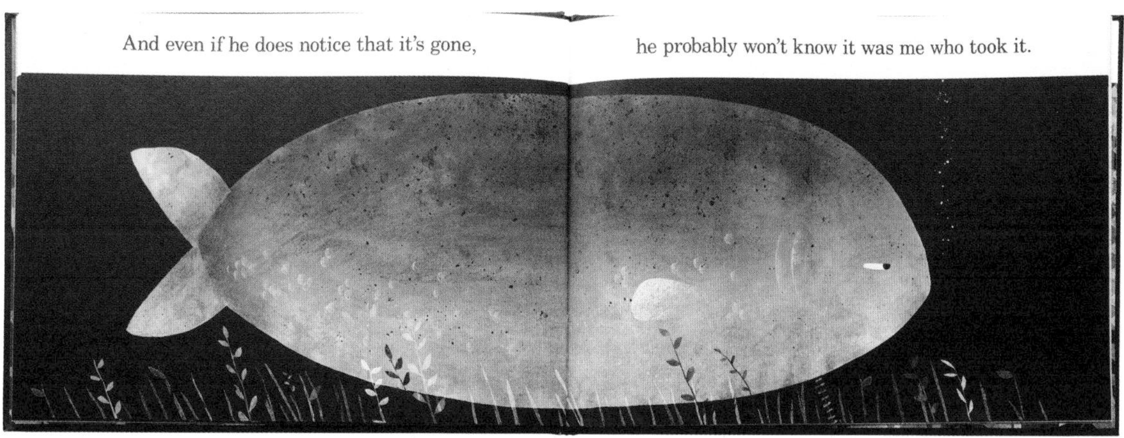

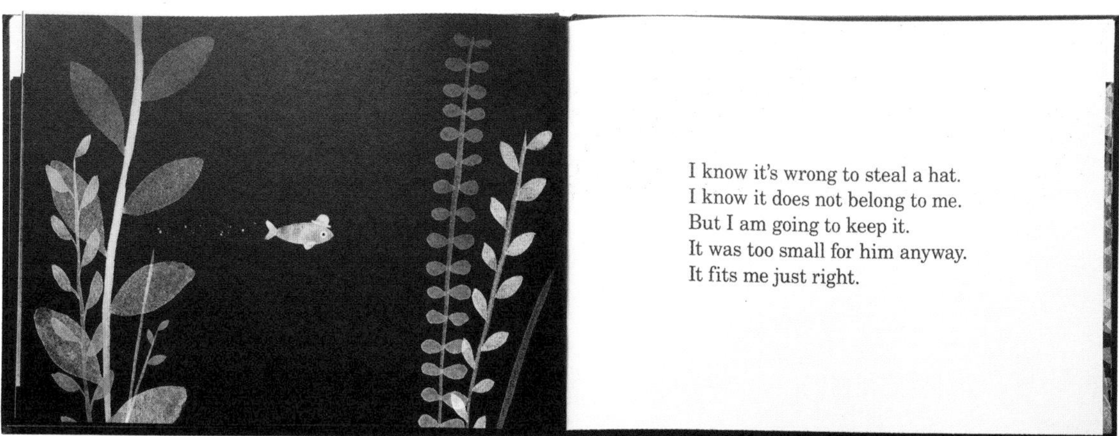

Nobody will ever find me.

The other story that was a big influence was Alfred Hitchcock's *Psycho*. The first half of the film is basically about guiltily running away, and getting tripped up in small ways as you go. Even though she doesn't meet her end directly because of what she did, it did make it more acceptable to the audience that she was on the run instead of just an innocent lady who needed a place to stay. The little fish's punishment is outsized compared to his crime, but he did have something coming.

The other piece from *Psycho* is the weird silence the film has in it after the main character has been killed. Even though people continue to talk and the movie continues to roll along, there's a weird void feeling to it now that she's gone. The idea for doing it in monologue came from the Poe story, but the idea for ending that monologue three spreads before the book was over came from *Psycho*.

I Want My Hat Back and *This Is Not My Hat* were done roughly a year apart. When Candlewick bought *I Want My Hat Back* they gave me a contract for three books. Whether it was the contract or the more general idea of a trilogy I'm not sure, but for some reason I always wanted to do a third book on the theme (now that there was a theme).

This third book turned out to be much harder to pin down. The second book had been done largely in reaction to the first one. It is the same trim size turned on its side, it is light shapes on a dark background rather than dark shapes on light, it is about a thief rather than somebody getting robbed, and it is done in monologue instead of dialogue. Since they are opposites in all of these ways, I couldn't figure out what the third book was supposed to do for a long time.

One thing I thought a third book could do is feature an ending where nobody ended up with the hat in question. Since both the previous books had established that you could be killed for stealing a hat, I thought a natural conclusion might be some sort of apocalyptic battle royale where everyone is killed in pursuit of the hat and nobody gets it.

The story I tried the most versions of along these lines was actually called *We Found A Hat*. The idea behind the title was that this book would be written as a group speaking in unison. The group would seem solid in their words, but you would see the fraying in the pictures and attitudes of the characters. There were a lot of variations on the story, but most of them included two or three characters standing around a hat they had found in the snow. They each tried it on in succession, coming to the conclusion that each of them liked it and wanted it. After a quick discussion about how the only fair thing to do would be to leave it and keep moving since they couldn't all three have one, they promptly sat down and just looked at it, for fear if any of them left first, the one who was left behind would claim the hat.

Eventually it would start to snow and the hat would be buried, and finally so would the unmoving creatures. The book ended with just a page of white, with everyone under the snow. I liked the setting, and I liked the idea of ending on a blank spread, but it didn't work. Everyone dying at the end of the story came off as didactic and cold. It took a long time and a lot of drafts to make sure there was no way to do it, but eventually I gave up on this version of the story altogether.

Many different stories and scenarios later, I came back to the title, but tried a version of the story where the characters genuinely liked each other. This version started almost exactly the same way, only instead of sitting and having a stand-off, the two turtles really do move away from the hat.

The second part of the book about them watching the sunset together shows that one of the turtles is still preoccupied with the thought of it. The third part of the book is set at night and has the tempted turtle almost steal the hat while the other is sleeping...

But, in a very strange coincidence, the turtle dream idea from the draft of the night time deer book almost five years before saves the day, and they float off into the stars together instead.

This third book, at least the writing of it, was the strangest and most meandering of all of them, but it taught me a lot about how much the process can change an idea if you let it. Up until this book, if an idea didn't work I didn't think there was much I could do to salvage it, and I would give it up and try something completely different.

But this book was at least partially salvaged from a number of old ideas that didn't have anything to do with each other at first, and it's been very relieving to see that this can lead to a book that I am just as happy with as a book that came by the other processes I've tried before.

For that reason I think this last one is my favourite of the series, though that may just be because it's such a relief to have finished it.

Suzy Lee

KOREA

Suzy Lee graduated from Seoul National University with a BFA in Painting, before heading to London to pursue a Masters in Book Arts at Camberwell College of Arts. Since then, she's created a selection of award-winning picturebooks which have been published around the world. Suzy lives and works in Seoul.

In this chapter, Suzy talks about how she made *Shadow*, the third title in her hugely successful *The Border Trilogy*. This inventive picturebook, which celebrates the power of imagination, was a New York Times Best Illustrated Book of the Year.

Suzy: I love everything about a 'book'. I love the great story in the book and I love the book as an object. The physical elements of the book are part of the story itself in some of my previous books.

The shape of *Mirror* (Corraini, 2003) is vertical like a typical full-length mirror, and it opens to the side.

The shape of *Wave* (Chronicle Books, 2008) is horizontal like the wide open sea, and it opens to the side too.

These two books are the same size and they share the same idea: the centre binding line between the double-page spreads of the book works as a border between fantasy and reality, physically as well as metaphorically. I wanted to make one more book to complete what was to become *The Border Trilogy*.

So what form was left?

"What if the shape of the third book is horizontal just like *Wave*, but the book opens in a different direction?" I thought.

Sometimes, the motivation for creating a book can come from the conditions of the book's structural form and not only from literary subjects.

I asked myself some more questions: "What if I make a book that opens from bottom to top? What if I create a top world and a bottom world which is divided by the border of fantasy and reality? What if a child plays in her own world, and her imaginary creations come alive on the other side of the world?" All of these "what if" ideas connected to one another, and I realised what the subject would be for the final book of the trilogy: shadows.

The shadow is an attractive subject. It is black, flat and mysterious. It doesn't have a face but we know that it is our reflected-self. I started making notes and thumbnail sketches immediately. [p.93]

Here's a translation of some of the notes from my sketchbook: 'The myth of Narcissus / "Dinner's ready!" Mum called. The child went out of the room. But what if the shadow of the child couldn't catch up? What if the shadow was the other being from the start? / Wendy sewing a shadow onto Peter Pan's foot / *Mystery and Melancholy of a Street* by Giorgio de Chirico'.

In the dark shed, with the click of a light bulb, a girl's imagination also lights up. She creates many shadows and plays with them... I started drawing the images. In *Mirror* and *Wave* I used charcoal, and I decided to use it in this book too. Charcoal displays two traits simultaneously: the linearity of clear strong lines and the dynamic sense of volume through finger-blurring effects.

6235 4981

'shadow'

그림자 — 거울 그림자 / 물 그림자

앞으로 비치는 vertical
뒤로 비치는

가로수의 허공에서 내린 비
— 웅덩이가 생기고 거기에 비친 그림자.

『그림자가 ... 』

'frame 밖에' 있을 것 같은 그림자.

커지는 그림자.

J.M. Barrie - Peter Pan.

그림자는 ... 아닐 수도.

45

Melancholy and Mistery of a street
giorgio de chirico

How to make the shadows then? How to make proper textured shadows that could go with the girl's rough charcoal lines?

A shadow traces the contour of something, and I felt that drawing by hand wouldn't express its distinctive lines. I had to think of another way to express the shadows while still maintaining their flat nature. Stencil seemed to be a good solution. I cut all the characters out from the stencil papers. After cutting around the shadow outlines one by one, my fingers wound up curved in the other direction.

I played around with spray paint. Spray paint is a flexible medium. When sprayed on paper that has been fixed in place, the spray offers clear outlines; when the paper is slightly lifted when spraying, the shadow's movement and perspective becomes remarkable.

Next, I built up all the drawings and shadows together, digitally. Then I added the colour. I chose yellow because it makes black stand out beautifully and clearly. Yellow shows the area of fantasy.

Back to the story. The girl has fun with the shadows she created. But the mischievous wolf attacks her and she runs away to the bottom world of shadows. And then, with the help of friends, she scares the wolf and the wolf bursts into tears. But in fact, the wolf is also the girl herself. Everyone opens their hearts easily.

The yellow that had existed only in the shadow world gradually crosses the border.

When *Shadow* got published, it was great to hear the readers' different ways of reading it.

Some said that you need to read it on your lap. If you place it at 90 degrees, the shadows look more convincing, as if they are cast on the floor.

Some said that you have to see both pages together to see the real and imaginary world at the same time.

Some said that you have to keep turning the book around. By rotating the book, you can even choose the part of the story that you want to see first. All methods of reading are totally possible because it's a 'book'.

The most interesting feedback I've ever had was from a girl in kindergarten. She liked the all-black double-page spreads the most. Why? Because when she casually flipped the pages, she saw another shadow through the black page as the light was behind it. She was able to catch the other shadow in the blink of an eye. Marvellous!

The readers always tell me their own method of reading books. And I believe that's the charm of wordless picturebooks.

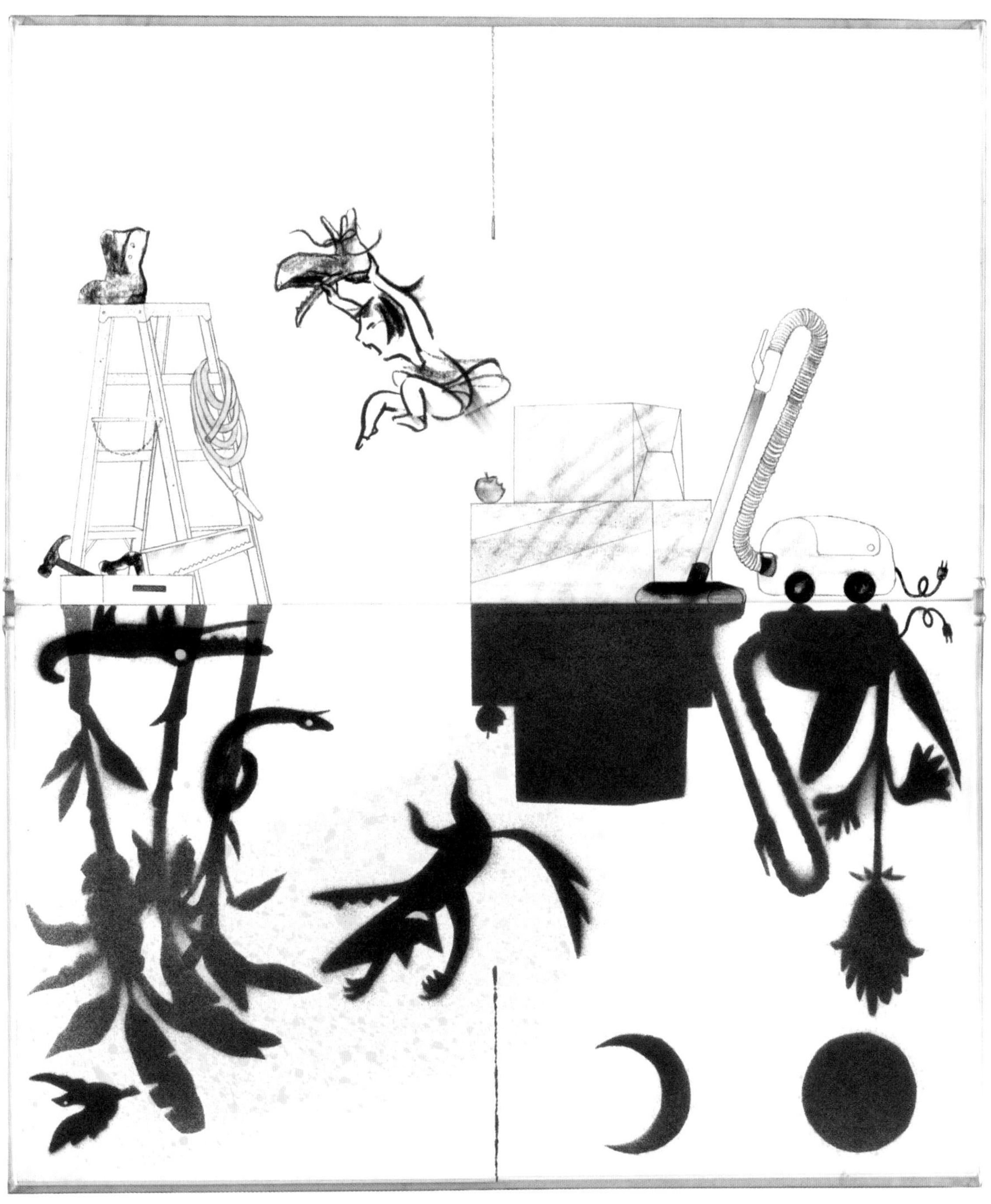

Bernardo P. Carvalho

PORTUGAL

Bernardo P. Carvalho is a graduate of the Lisbon Faculty of Fine Arts and co-founder of the highly innovative publishing house Planeta Tangerina. He's received many awards for his work, including a CJ Picture Book Award, the National Illustration Award, and several wins and Special Mentions in the BolognaRagazzi Awards.

In this chapter, Bernardo talks about the creation of *Olhe, por favor, não viu uma luzinha a piscar? / Corre, coelhinho, corre! (Follow the Firefly / Run, Rabbit, Run!)*, an ingenious picturebook which can be read both backwards and forwards.

Bernardo: This book's story started a long time ago, when here at Planeta Tangerina we started with this idea of trying to tell parallel stories and different things that take place at the same time, in the same book.

I believe that being publishers as well as illustrators gives us a great advantage in being able to take chances and make books as we wish to make them – about whichever topics we wish – rather than merely working on-demand.

With this comes the desire to explore and knead the book in a different way, to tell stories from left to right, from right to left, and both ways simultaneously.

Anything is allowed, except making folds, holes in the pages or pop-ups, because that's cheating (and very expensive).

When talking about *Follow the Firefly / Run, Rabbit, Run!*, it's impossible not to at least mention two other books: In *The World in a Second* (2006), we froze the world for one second and looked at the many things that happen at precisely that second, all around the world. And *Two Roads* (2009) is a book with two parallel stories that, in a similar way to *Follow the Firefly / Run, Rabbit, Run!*, move in opposite directions – but in this case with text and drawings overlaid and inverted.

In that sense, *Follow the Firefly / Run, Rabbit, Run!* is a sort of extension of the idea of telling things that are happening at exactly the same time, or as in this instance, two different stories that share the same stage, or one story that gives rise to another, or stories that latch onto one another in a never-ending loop.

PLANETA TANGERINA
OLHE, POR FAVOR, NÃO VIU UMA LUZINHA A PISCAR?
BERNARDO CARVALHO

When one ends, the next one starts – and it starts because the other one has ended. Confused? It sounds confusing when told this way, but it isn't. The most important thing was to get the reader to follow just one story without consciously being aware of the other one, or at least to make sure the other story didn't get in the way of the first one, and vice versa. As always, I ruminated over the idea for some time, making tons of small sequences in my sketchbooks and on spare pieces of paper or coffee napkins that I then subsequently lost here and there...

VIU UMA LUZINHA A PISCAR?
VISTE UMA LUZINHA A PISCAR?

FUGITIV
12
3

Due to my lack of discipline, or just because I enjoy experimenting, or for some other reason, I rarely reuse the same technique from one book to the next, and this one was no exception. That's why I decided to illustrate it with watercolour, which is something I'd never done before.

Techniques where patience and precision are paramount are not my strength, and I'm usually more restrained regarding excessive drawing and confusing scenes.

But in this case, I realised that it could actually come in handy, to sort of camouflage the other story hiding behind it.

With plainer colours and fewer details, it would have been harder to distance ourselves from the other story. In other words, for this book to work it was very important that the two stories be completely readable and autonomous, despite sharing the same set of pages and setting.

For two stories to share the same pages and setting, the challenge is more in the organisation and how to display the images within the frame, rather than in the illustration process itself.

Both narratives in this book are journeys in opposite directions: One from the forest to the city, the other from the city to the forest.

Follow the Firefly

In the first story, which begins at a barbecue around a campfire in the woods, we follow a firefly who's feeling sad because he doesn't have a blinking light to keep him company. And so he sets off alone on a long journey, asking (politely as only fireflies can be) the other animals that he meets along the way if they've "seen a little blinking light?"

All the directions he receives point him to the big city, where he finally meets and falls in love with a light that blinks: a traffic light.

Run, Rabbit, Run!

That reciprocated love between firefly and traffic light (now completely overrun with passion and blinking lights) causes a huge crash at the crossing, with several cars involved. Among these cars is a pickup truck belonging to a hunter of exotic animals. From the impact of the crash, the cage of one of the white bunnies opens and the bunny escapes. The hunter's guard dog was alert and notices this, and so begins an epic chase that leads them both from the city to the forest. In the forest, the bunny finds shelter on the back of his gorilla friend, and now the dog in turn finds himself alone and lost, far from home and not knowing his way back.

Luckily for the dog, our bunny is a pretty cool bunny and invites him to a barbecue with the rest of his friends – one of which is a firefly who's feeling sad because he doesn't have a blinking light to keep him company.

Isol

ARGENTINA

Isol (Marisol Misenta) is an Argentine pop singer, illustrator and picturebook maker. Since her first book was published in 1997, she's produced an impressive body of work and has won many awards. For her contribution to children's and young adult literature, Isol received the Astrid Lindgren Memorial Award in 2013.

In this chapter, Isol talks about the creation of *La bella Griselda (Beautiful Griselda)*. This striking picturebook about the pitfalls of narcissism was originally published in Spanish by Fondo de Cultura Económica, and has been translated into several languages.

Isol: This book was born from a popular phrase which is related to the idea of metaphorically losing one's head over someone. The literal illustration of this phrase, which is like a compliment when said of someone – she is so beautiful that everyone loses their head over her – was the trigger for the entire story of *Beautiful Griselda*.

The image of this situation seemed disturbing and comic to me, with the heads of the suitors rolling around her.

What would you do with so many heads?

Collect them? Something about the values of the perfect princess, of conquests for the ego, seemed to be stripped bare after continually drawing and taking to the extreme the situation where beauty never brings real happiness to its owner. The princess starts to wish she could find someone who doesn't succumb to her beauty, so she calls to a nearly-blind prince who will last at least a couple of hours – until the moment arrives in which the protagonist herself happily loses her own head when she becomes a mother.

The sketches were done in pencil, and I changed parts of the story as time went on after conversations with my friends and colleagues. My early sketches are very similar to some of the final illustrations.

The pages after Griselda loses her head were initially the most work for me, as finishing a story is always the most difficult part. Leaving a girl without a mother could be very sad, so I had to be delicate with the final illustrations.

The final phrase of the book is difficult to translate into some languages because it's a play on

La Bella Griselda
ISOL

words that only works in Latin languages: 'The daughter loves to assemble jigsaw puzzles'. In Spanish, 'jigsaw puzzles' is literally 'break heads', so for the English version I had to find another way.

With my books, I always work a lot on the text so that it's concise and powerful, and I do the same with the drawings.

Once I had finished the sketches, I took quite a while to find the right visual language for the book. I didn't have faith in the flowing and simple lines of the sketches, and I wanted to research other possibilities.

I tried ink sgraffito and oil pastels, but it started to lose fluidity and looked overdone. In the end, I returned to a line similar to that of the sketches, in which the expression of the characters was the most clear. But I had trouble developing the final drawings and their expression. I ended up working with pencil and pen on tracing paper.

Another challenge was having to draw scenes in which a lot was happening, and scenes with many people, which was something I hadn't done in my previous books. It was clear that I had to draw the interior of the palace where Griselda lived, or at least evoke it somehow. I worked with pastel on paper, then took photos and tried them out on the computer. There's so many options! Working with the computer can be a never-ending story. I had to simplify matters. I think it was for that reason that I finally decided to use only four colours in the entire book, and only Pantone colours, which are colours from a special international palette.

I've loved using solid colours ever since I did serigraphy (silkscreens) and etching, where the colours are applied separately.

I played with the transparencies and overlapping of the colours, and with the colours of the lines of the characters. I also had to learn how to work with separate inks. It took me a while but it was very interesting, and having those possibilities and limitations resolved other questions for me. I worked by using channels in Photoshop (not the standard CMYK colours).

For the first time, I used patterns taken from origami papers to make the costumes and the castle decorations, processing them and putting them into the drawing. I was also influenced by the floral designs of medieval tapestries, which were a great reference point as they've fascinated me for some time. In fact, I used a composition similar to that of the 15th century tapestry *The Lady and the Unicorn* for the front cover.

The great Paolo Uccello was a reference point for the knights, and I took photos of mosaics I have on the floor of my house and used them on the floor of Griselda's castle. And in the countryside background when Griselda is in the carriage, I needed the castles to be weighty and concrete, not light and movable like in my drawings. So I used real castles in the background of the illustration to give it strength. [pp.122–123]

Thanks to the time I dedicated to this book, I feel that it took on a coherent and strong aesthetic, without losing any of its freshness or humour.

Manuel Marsol

SPAIN

Manuel Marsol has degrees in Advertising and Audiovisual Communication, and a postgraduate diploma in Children's Book Illustration. His work has received much international acclaim, and his numerous awards include the Bologna International Prize for Illustration SM, Pépite in Montreuil, Amadora BD in Portugal, and a BolognaRagazzi.

In this chapter, Manuel talks about the creation of his stunning debut picturebook *Ahab y la ballena blanca (Ahab and the White Whale)*, which won the Edelvives International Picture Book Award in 2014. This poetic and beautifully illustrated story was inspired by *Moby Dick* and by Manuel's lifelong fascination and love for the ocean.

Manuel: *Ahab y la Ballena Blanca (Ahab and the White Whale)* is inspired by *Moby Dick*, and tells the story of a sailor obsessed with finding a whale that is, paradoxically, always in front of him. Ahab thinks that what he has in front of him is a strange warm iceberg, but in reality he is touching the great white whale.

This is a story about obsession and the mysteries of the sea.

As a child, I would spend the summer on the Mar Menor and dive for hours with my sister, surrounded by fish and jellyfish, experimenting with a mix of fear, excitement and happiness.

Then we would paint everything we had seen underwater with our parents. Onto the paper we would glue seashells and even dried seahorses we found on the sand.

Moby Dick, a book I really love, was the excuse to make a book related to those memories about the fantastic and everyday side of the sea, which sums up the mystery of life quite well: it is within our reach and we admire it, but it holds things that we will never understand and that scare us. Beauty and fear. It may seem calm on the surface, but what battles are fought down there? When I was a child, the sea was a door to the unknown; what was the difference between a jellyfish infestation and an alien invasion?

Memories are not enough to tell a story. This is where the difficulties start! I believe firmly in the capacity of thinking through drawing. At first, I am not sure where I am going, setting out on a series of emotions, landscapes or atmospheres. To me, this is absolutely essential to the development of the story.

PEQUOD

For example, I began drawing a giant white whale rising to the surface, like an island with palm trees, which is another engraved childhood memory about a book we had at home: *Sol Solet* by the theatre group Els Comediants (recipient of the Critici in Herba award at the Bologna Children's Book Fair in 1985).

Then I drew a cliff in the shape of a whale's head. At that point, I still had no idea what the story would be. I kept on drawing many scenes of whales 'hidden' in the landscape, along with loose ideas that did not fit in what would later become the picturebook. But some other ideas are almost intact in the final version.

Then I thought it would be fun to see Ahab obsessed with searching for something he always had right under his nose. And so I realised the connection between one of the biggest themes in *Moby Dick* (obsession) and what I was doing. Besides, it was linked to my creative process: we are often sitting so close to the solution that we can't see it. Sometimes, a few steps back from the fog are enough to realise that it's actually a whale.

'Accidents' are a very important part of my work, but there is also plenty of research: I read monographs on *Moby Dick*, I rewatched John Huston's movie, reread passages from the book and references on the internet...

Everything contributes to producing a sudden spark. Some people work with a very clear idea of the story they want to tell and how they want to tell it before even starting. In my case, I let my obsessions, intuition and research do the first part of the work. The rest is rational; everything must make sense, and

Un encuentro entre Moby
y Ahab.

Ballena
Blanca

le
lleva

FINA

LA GRAN
BALLENA
BLANCA

X No?

that is where insecurities and obstacles come in. There is no straight path. It is a matter of winning small battles, of making mistakes until you correct them, be it because you saw them or because your editors, your girlfriend or your friends saw them.

One of these battles is the tone of the illustrations. This is a task I begin before having a story, whether a test or a potential final illustration. It is very hard to visualise the rest of the book graphically until you find that one image that you know is the right one. I had no doubts after I had digitally retouched the below drawing, which was done on paper with Chinese ink, collage, watercolours, pencils and plastic emulsion paint.

I like to try things out in Photoshop after scanning. I like to change the levels, the tone, or switch the colours. In this case, my own drawing had surprised me, as if I had not created it myself! This is why I always say that we must be open to the accidents in the process – to things we had not foreseen – because they provide a freshness that is impossible to achieve intentionally. When I saw that night with its azure trees, another rush of childhood memories came back to me about pirates and the sea. Fear and fascination. Like the sense of mystery I felt when I played Monkey Island on the PC.

For the final illustration, I just modified the character and enlarged it to a double-page spread.

After this discovery, many nocturnal or underwater illustrations were conceived in reverse. I mean, I thought of which colours were necessary so that

when I inverted them I would get the desired result. For example, if I wanted a red octopus, I drew it in blue. The original drawings look like they were made by someone who is colour blind!

Many good ideas only show up while you are facing specific issues. In the first depictions of the Kraken, who was to steal Ahab's leg, I wanted to make the intertwining tentacles stand out, taking up the entire page. But I didn't want it to look dramatic. So I needed a fun idea, and I thought I could make the octopus look like a giant hand. Now it was an octopus with a sense of humour. I drew it twenty times, changing tentacles here and there, until the image worked as a hand without stopping being an octopus. [pp.132–133]

The upside is that during this process, enriching details tend to pop up, like giving the octopus an eel-ring!

I presented the text (another of the picturebook's big battles) as a project for the Edelvives International Picture Book Award, and it was different to the text in the final book. This was because months passed between me receiving the award and the final artwork delivery. During that time, I had the chance to rework it, but it wasn't until almost the day before delivery that I rewrote it from beginning to end! The story was the same; the problem was that the voice I had used before was not quite right.

Originally, someone else was telling us Ahab's story. The captain said things out loud; he complained and grumbled. You might know the feeling that when something doesn't work, you can just sense it. You might not know exactly how to fix it, but you know that something is not right. And when you finally put your finger on it, and you know what to do, you feel like screaming for joy.

So the text was too flashy, every line wanted to be funny, and it often repeated what we already saw in the images. It did not fit with the poetry of the illustrations; they asked for peace, they wanted us to observe the infinity of the details and to think. I began by reducing the amount of text, but it was not enough. One morning, I thought, I'll tell the story in the first person, as if I was Ahab. And suddenly the screaming gave way to the silence – that is, the mystery, the interpretations and the multiple readings. I rewrote it in one morning. It almost wrote itself. And this happens after a lot of work: everything tidies itself up without warning! But I had actually been rewriting the story in my head for a long time.

QUO

Regarding the colour, my reference was John Huston's film of *Moby Dick*. I liked the classical touch it achieved with such a limited palette. Despite that it is in colour, we get the feeling we are watching a black-and-white movie.

As I moved further through the process, together with my editors, we realised it would be interesting to add some amazing glints of sea life colour. I think the picturebook has a good balance between the classical and let's call it hallucinogenic sides of the ocean floor.

Many people ask me about the textures. These are inspired by the chipped paint on fishermen's boats, seaweed on sunken bricks, fish scales, seashells, etc. As a child I would stare at the seaweed and almost touch the ocean floor with my nose. I also remember the feeling of holding a fish in my hand: the texture of its raspy skin.

On the other hand, some of the textures are also greatly influenced by an abstract painter from Madrid called López-Soldado. I was brought up surrounded by his paintings because he was my father's best friend. I spent a few months painting with him and he taught me some of his techniques, based on mixtures which give random results that have always interested me (like oil with acrylic, water with Chinese ink, etc).

His amazing world fascinated me to the extent of running my hand over his paintings. This is why I like it when I see people running their hands over the pages of my book, as if they expect to feel something coarse – like the feeling I had as a child when I held a fish in my hand.

le Chuck

Johanna Schaible

SWITZERLAND

Johanna Schaible is an artist whose work moves along the borders of illustration, art, and design. She has a degree in Illustration and Visual Communication from the Lucerne School of Art and Design, and she was one of the first members of Bolo Klub, a collective supporting an emerging generation of picturebook makers in Switzerland.

In this chapter, Johanna talks about her incredible debut picturebook *Once upon a time there was and will be so much more*. In the first dPICTUS Unpublished Picturebook Showcase in 2019, this project was voted for by 23 of the 30 publishers on the jury, acquired by Lilla Piratförlaget, and then published as a co-edition in nine languages.

Johanna: I will tell you about my picturebook *Once upon a time there was and will be so much more*. The book takes us on a journey through time. It begins in the distant past, catches up to the present halfway through, and then leads us with questions into the future.

Time is depicted in a special way. The pages of the book get smaller as we draw closer to the present and grow larger again as we move into the future.

Back when I made my first dummy books, it was hard to believe that it would turn into a real book one day. For a long time, I heard from the publishing world that it is very difficult to produce a book like this and it would be even harder, if not impossible, to find a publisher who would take the risk, effort and cost to produce it.

It took some time, but it happened in the end!

The book's journey started with Bolo Klub, which was founded several years ago by the Swiss illustration duo It's Raining Elephants. Bolo Klub supports illustrators in completing a picture-book, and provides networking opportunities with professionals from the publishing world.

I had the chance to take part in the first edition from 2018–2019. We were a wonderful group of fifteen illustrators that came together once a month to push our book projects forward and to benefit from each other's feedback.

I do a lot of projects moving between art and illustration. To make a picturebook sounded very challenging to me, especially because I rarely work on narrative.

I'm attracted by books with exciting formats, and I wasn't up for creating a regular one.

Millions of years ago, dinosaurs lived on Earth.

Yesterday, the weather was stormy.

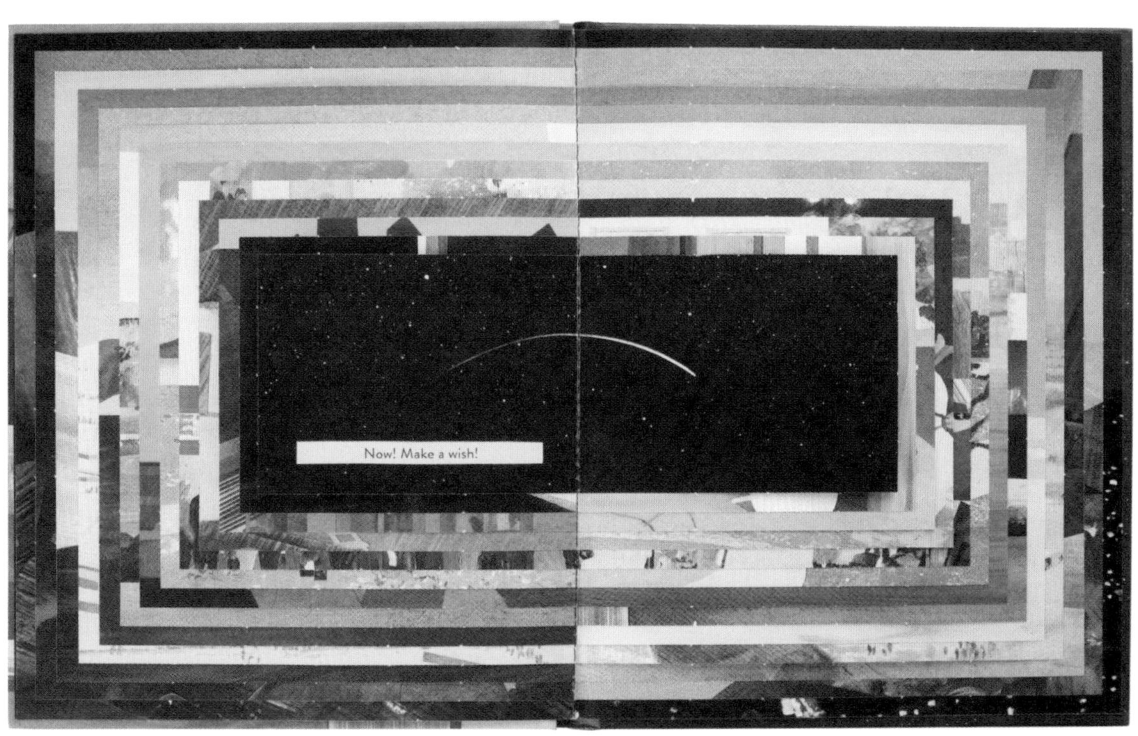
Now! Make a wish!

Will you have children one day?

My starting points were thematically very open and global. My keywords, for example, were 'night', 'air' and 'time'.

With the aim to really make progress on our projects, Bolo Klub spent a working weekend together. Besides the working, it was so enriching to exchange thoughts and ideas. In a creative process, we all face similar challenges. At this stage, I was working on two ideas. The first idea was a zoom, starting far away and coming in close to one child. The second idea was a dummy book with the topic 'time'.

Combining the two ideas was the turning point. I had finally found the theme and concept that I was looking for.

I often work with collage and painting for my illustrations. I also do my sketches using this technique because I want to see the atmosphere of an image and idea straight away.

To start with, I made some little sketches the size of postcards. [p.143] In this case I work more roughly, and I appreciate the liveliness that inhabits these sketches. I feel comfortable working quite fast. It helps me to develop the images intuitively.

Then I made a lot of little dummy books to observe what happened while turning the pages. I realised that I had to find simple sentences that gave the timeline and structure to the book. [pp.144–145]

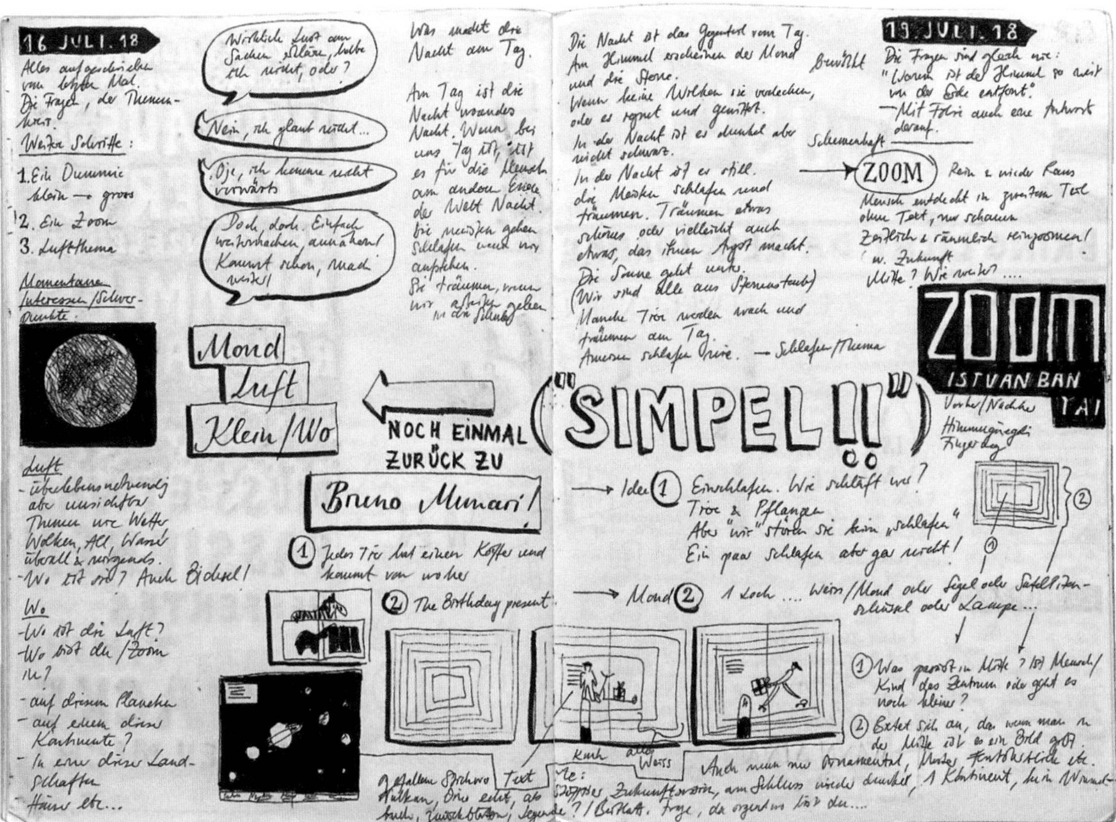

RIGHT PAGE PHOTOGRAPH BY EDI ETTLIN

Es war einmal und wird noch viel

Für die Erwachsenen von morgen und die Kinder von gestern

In einem Monat kreist der Mond um die Erde.
23 Uhr
3 Uhr
7 Uhr
1 Uhr
11 Uhr
5 Uhr
6 Uhr
10 uhr
8 Uhr
14 Uhr
12 Uhr
4 Uhr
24 Uhr
9Uhr
13 Uhr
15 Uhr
16 Uhr
17 Uhr
GLEICH
GROSS

Alongside the development of a coherent journey through time, I had to think about the feasibility of my idea. When I did my little dummy books, they were very imprecise. It was only when I started to measure the pages and make examples of the real book size that I realised that my pages didn't just get smaller, but their format changed completely. The format changes from a more common picturebook size to a wide panorama format, and then back again. To be sure about the size, it helped me to use frames that I put over my collages, to be able to change and move elements until the end.

With Bolo Klub and my dummy book, I travelled to the Bologna Children's Book Fair 2019. In Bologna, some publishers told me they were interested. But I never heard from them again.

It was another call that boosted this project. I sent my dummy book to the first edition of the dPICTUS Unpublished Picturebook Showcase in 2019, and was thrilled when I heard that 23 of the 30 publishers on the jury voted independently for my project. It made me very happy because it showed me that, even if that didn't mean that they would publish it, my book was touching them in some way.

It was also through The Unpublished Picturebook Showcase that my book project found the publisher that accepted the big challenge of making it a reality. I was very lucky with my Swedish editor Erik Titusson from Lilla Piratförlaget and Sam McCullen from dPICTUS on the graphic design. In our collaboration, I felt a big trust in me and my work.

My creative process for this project was similar to how it very often is for me: Some pictures came easily and stayed very close to the original sketch, but for some of the other pictures, I had to do them over and over again until they felt right to me.

With my technique of mixing painting and cutouts, I really like to develop scenes and create atmospheres. To show humans inhabiting these scenes was a challenge in the beginning. It became easier after I decided to paint the figures at a larger size. For some images I made the whole setting first. Then I cut out the figures and inserted them digitally.

Whenever I got stuck, it helped to go outside and take photos of the daily life around me.

To make this book was a precious experience to me. The companionship and support from Bolo Klub was very helpful and enriching. On this journey, I've had the chance to meet a lot of inspiring people who shared their knowledge and offered me their help. I'm so thankful to all of them, and especially to my closest allies and friends who support me in all of my projects.

I hope that this book will offer to people of all ages the possibility to talk about what kind of future we imagine and want to build together.

Online content

Blexbolex
picturebookmakers.com/blexbolex

Shaun Tan
shauntan.net
instagram.com/shauncytan
picturebookmakers.com/shauntan

Chris Haughton
chrishaughton.com
instagram.com/chrishaughton
picturebookmakers.com/chrishaughton

Jon Klassen
writershouseart.com/jon-klassen
instagram.com/jonklassen
picturebookmakers.com/jonklassen

Bernardo P. Carvalho
planetatangerina.com
instagram.com/planetatangerina
picturebookmakers.com/bernardopcarvalho

Manuel Marsol
manuelmarsol.com
instagram.com/manuelmarsol
picturebookmakers.com/manuelmarsol

Eva Lindström
instagram.com/lindstrom1237
picturebookmakers.com/evalindstrom

Beatrice Alemagna
beatricealemagna.com
instagram.com/beatricealemagna
picturebookmakers.com/beatricealemagna

Kitty Crowther
kittycrowther.com
instagram.com/kittycrowther
picturebookmakers.com/kittycrowther

Suzy Lee
suzyleebooks.com
instagram.com/suzyleebooks
picturebookmakers.com/suzylee

Isol
instagram.com/isolmisenta
picturebookmakers.com/isol

Johanna Schaible
johannaschaible.ch
instagram.com/johannaschaible
picturebookmakers.com/johannaschaible

Picturebook Makers blog + gallery
blog.picturebookmakers.com
gallery.picturebookmakers.com

The Unpublished Picturebook Showcase
dpictus.com/unpublished

Pitch-Your-Books
dpictus.com/pitch-your-books

dPICTUS platform
dpictus.com

100 Outstanding Picturebooks
dpictus.com/100-outstanding-picturebooks

Other
instagram.com/picturebookmakers
facebook.com/picturebookmakers

ILLUSTRATION BY MANUEL MARSOL

WELLS FARGO & CO.

SKETCH BY KITTY CROWTHER